USING A
WHEELCHAIR

BY HARRIET BRUNDLE

KidHaven
PUBLISHING

HUMAN BODY HELPERS

Published in 2019 by
KidHaven Publishing, an Imprint of Greenhaven Publishing, LLC
353 3rd Avenue
Suite 255
New York, NY 10010

Designer: Danielle Rippengill
Editor: Kirsty Holmes

Photo credits: *All images are courtesy of Shutterstock.com, unless otherwise specified. With thanks to Getty Images, Thinkstock Photo and iStockphoto. Front Cover & 1 – Visual Generation, mei yanotai, Beatriz Gascon J, NikaMooni, Milan M. Images used on every spread – grmarc, Beatriz Gascon J, NikaMooni, Visual Generation, mei yanotai. 2 – Jane Kelly, svtdesign, Nadia Snopek. 5 – Sudowoodo. 9 – Nadia Snopek. 10 – SunshineVector, hvostik. 13 – MicroOne, Evellean, Iconic Bestiary, FoxyImage, lenoleum. 14 – svtdesign, Nadia Snopek. 15 – Jane Kelly, monkographic. 17 – Jane Kelly, monkographic. 18 & 19 – lenoleum. 19 – VikiVector. 20 – Oxy_gen. 23 – Andrew Rybalko.*

All facts, statistics, web addresses and URLs in this book were verified as valid and accurate at time of writing. No responsibility for any changes to external websites or references can be accepted by either the author or publisher.

Cataloging-in-Publication Data

Names: Brundle, Harriet.
Title: Using a wheelchair / Harriet Brundle.
Description: New York : KidHaven Publishing, 2019. | Series: Human body helpers | Includes glossary and index.
Identifiers: ISBN 9781534529557 (pbk.) | ISBN 9781534529571 (library bound) | ISBN 9781534529564 (6 pack) | ISBN 9781534529588 (ebook)
Subjects: LCSH: Wheelchairs–Juvenile literature. | Bones–Wounds and injuries–Juvenile literature. | Fractures in children–Juvenile literature.
Classification: LCC RD757.W4 B77 2019 | DDC 617'.033–dc23

Printed in the United States of America

CPSIA compliance information: Batch #BW19KL· For further information contact Greenhaven Publishing LLC, New York, New York at 1-844-317-7404.

Please visit our website, www.greenhavenpublishing.com. For a free color catalog of all our high-quality books, call toll free 1-844-317-7404 or fax 1-844-317-7405.

CONTENTS

Words that look like **this** can be found in the glossary on page 24.

YOUR BONES

BONES ... WE ALL HAVE THEM. BUT WHY DO WE NEED THEM?

All our different bones form our skeleton, which is the framework for our body. Our skeleton has the important job of supporting our bodies and protecting our **organs**.

Hi! I'm Betsy Bone. I'm your tibia, or shinbone.

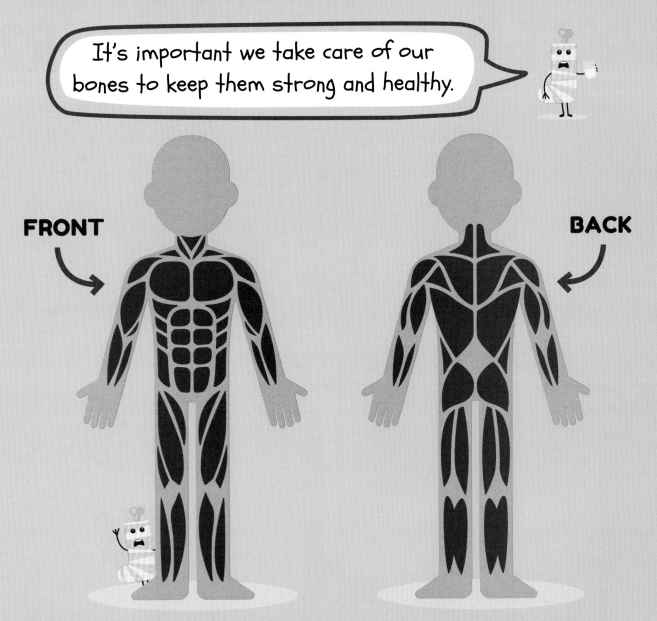

Without our skeleton, we wouldn't be able to stand up straight or move around very well. Our **muscles** are attached to our bones, and together they allow us to move as we do.

WHAT IS A WHEELCHAIR?

A wheelchair is a chair that has been fitted with wheels that allow a person to move around. Some wheelchairs need to be pushed and others work **electronically**.

Some wheelchairs that need to be pushed have handles so someone can stand behind and push the chair along.

Other types are made so that you can move yourself around. Electronic wheelchairs are moved around with **controls**.

WHY MIGHT I NEED A WHEELCHAIR?

A person might need to use a wheelchair because they are sick, they have hurt themselves, or they have a **disability**.

I'm here to help.

Some people may need to use a wheelchair for their whole lives, while others only need a wheelchair for a shorter amount of time.

You might need a wheelchair if you have hurt yourself, especially your legs, ankles, or feet.

You may need a wheelchair until you can put weight on the injury.

HOW DO WHEELCHAIRS WORK?

Electric wheelchairs and those that need pushing have some differences in how they look and the way they work.

The controls usually have a part that you push in the direction you want to move.

If you have an electric wheelchair, you can use the controls to move the wheelchair in the direction you want to go.

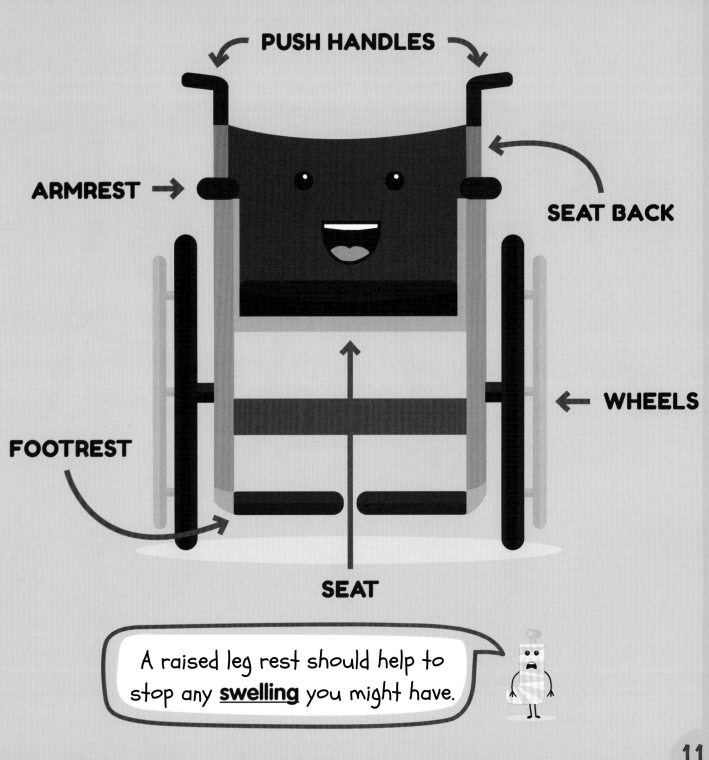

PUSH HANDLES

ARMREST →

SEAT BACK

FOOTREST

WHEELS ←

SEAT

A raised leg rest should help to stop any **swelling** you might have.

There are lots of different types of wheelchairs. They all have different features that suit a person's needs. Some have larger wheels at the back, which makes them easier to move around.

Different types of wheelchairs might have different styles of arm, foot, or leg rests, so it's important that your wheelchair is comfortable for you. You may also need a removable seat, which can make the chair more comfortable, too.

WHAT HAPPENS AT THE HOSPITAL?

If you hurt yourself, an adult might think that you need to visit the hospital to have your injury checked.

Don't panic, X-rays don't hurt at all!

If the doctor or nurse thinks you might have broken a bone, you will usually be sent for an **X-ray**.

If your bone is broken, it might need to be put into a **<u>cast</u>**.

That's where I come in.

You may need to be careful that you don't put any weight on the broken bone, or it may be too difficult to walk. In these cases, you might need a wheelchair to help you get around.

WHAT TO EXPECT

In the days after you have broken a bone, it might be painful and you might feel very aware of your cast if you have one.

After a few weeks, you'll feel more used to wearing a cast and you should feel less pain.

If you're in lots of pain, be sure to tell an adult.

You might need to ask an adult to help you if you need to get out of your wheelchair.

You will usually be told how long you'll need a wheelchair for.

You will be shown how to use your wheelchair safely, but you might find it a bit difficult to move around at first.

DOS AND DON'TS

DO make sure if you have stopped your wheelchair that you put on the brakes.

DON'T sit on the edge of the seat. Make sure you're seated in the center of the chair.

Ask an adult if you need help with the footrests.

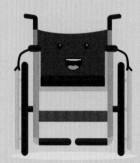

DO make sure you lift the footrests before you try to get out of your wheelchair, otherwise you could trip over them.

DON'T put anything heavy, like a bag, on the back of the chair. It might tip backwards!

DO try to keep your cast clean.

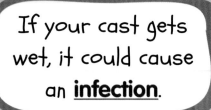

If your cast gets wet, it could cause an **<u>infection</u>**.

DON'T get your cast wet. You may need a special plastic cover to make sure you don't get your cast wet while you're washing.

DO tell an adult if your cast feels very uncomfortable, as you may need to go back to the hospital.

DON'T put anything inside your cast. Even if your skin feels itchy, make sure you don't try pushing anything under the cast to scratch yourself.

You might not be able to get the object out again and it could cause **irritation**.

LIFE AFTER YOUR WHEELCHAIR

ONCE IT'S SAFE FOR YOU TO START PUTTING WEIGHT ON YOUR INJURY, YOU NO LONGER NEED YOUR WHEELCHAIR.

I'm much better now, Winnie. Thanks for your help!

You're welcome, Betsy.

You might still have a cast or support on your injury for a while longer, though.

Although your injury may have healed so that you no longer need your wheelchair, others may need their wheelchair for the rest of their lives.

It's important to be **considerate** of those who use a wheelchair.

GLOSSARY

CAST	a hard covering made to help body parts heal
CONSIDERATE	showing care and thought
CONTROLS	tools used for moving a machine
DISABILITY	when someone can't do some things because of a long-term injury, illness or medical condition
ELECTRONICALLY	by means of electronic machine or device
INFECTION	any disease caused by germs
IRRITATION	discomfort
MUSCLES	parts of the body that are made of tissue and help us move
ORGANS	parts of the body that have special jobs
SWELLING	the enlargement of a body part
X-RAY	a photograph of the inside of your body

INDEX